CROSSING THE BORDER

BECOMING A U.S. CITIZEN

CATHLEEN SMALL

LUCENT
PRESS

Published in 2018 by
Lucent Press, an Imprint of Greenhaven Publishing, LLC
353 3rd Avenue
Suite 255
New York, NY 10010

Produced for Lucent by Calcium
Designer: Jeni Child
Picture researcher: Rachel Blount
Editors: Sarah Eason and Nancy Dickmann

Picture credits: Cover: Shutterstock: Bill Dowling (main), Vinokurov Kirill (top); Inside: Library of Congress: Theodore R. Davis 14, P. Frenzeny 11br; Shutterstock: 1000 Words 60–61, Diego G Diaz 40–41, Dragon Images 27, 28, Onur Ersin 9, Everett Historical 5, 17, 18, 19, 21t, Featureflash Photo Agency 33, Filipe Frazao 31, Len Green 58, Hayk_Shalunts 39, Holbox 4, Andrea Izzotti 8, A Katz 51, Kdonmuang 50, Mimagephotography 55, Leigh Anne Meeks 10–11, Olga Popova 32, Prazis 56–57, Joseph Sohm 49, Wavebreakmedia 54, Welcomia 24, Lukasz Z 29, Zerbor 36–37; Wikimedia Commons: Gulbenk 44, Håkan Dahlström 35, Dorothea Lange/U.S. National Archives and Records Administration 13b, 13t, Russell Lee 20–21, Gerald Nino/CPB 46–47, NPS Photo by Michael Quinn 52, Ferdinand Schmutzer Restored by Adam Cuerden 42, Cecil Stoughton, White House Press Office (WHPO) 23, John Trumbull 6–7.

Cataloging-in-Publication Data

Names: Small, Cathleen.
Title: Becoming a U.S. citizen / Cathleen Small.
Description: New York : Lucent Press, 2018. | Series: Crossing the border | Includes index.
Identifiers: ISBN 9781534562271 (library bound) | ISBN 9781534562288 (ebook) | ISBN 9781534562769 (paperback)
Subjects: LCSH: Citizenship--United States--Juvenile literature. | Naturalization--United States--Juvenile literature.
Classification: LCC KF4700.S63 2018 | DDC 342.7308'3--dc23

Printed in the United States of America

CPSIA compliance information: Batch #CW18KL: For further information contact Greenhaven Publishing LLC, New York, New York at 1-844-317-7404.

Please visit our website, www.greenhavenpublishing.com. For a free color catalog of all our high-quality books, call toll free 1-844-317-7404 or fax 1-844-317-7405.

CONTENTS

CHAPTER 1

U.S. CITIZENSHIP: A SHORT HISTORY

"Give me your tired, your poor,
Your huddled masses yearning to breathe free,
The wretched refuse of your teeming shore.
Send these, the homeless, tempest-tost to me,
I lift my lamp beside the golden door!"

The words of poet Emma Lazarus are inscribed on a plaque on the inner wall of the Statue of Liberty's pedestal. The statue, America's iconic symbol of freedom, was seen by immigrants arriving to the United States' eastern shore in New York by boat. Lazarus's words reflect the idea that the United States was a refuge for people from other countries who were seeking a new home. Sometimes the immigrants were fleeing war, poverty, or other strife, and sometimes they were simply seeking work and a better standard of life. But they shared in common a desire to find in the United States their new home.

The Statue of Liberty wasn't dedicated until 1886. Lazarus's words, first written in 1883, were inscribed on the statue's plaque in 1903. But the spirit of the words and the statue were present years—even centuries—before. The United States has always been a land of immigrants, which has led to it being the cultural melting pot it is today.

 The Statue of Liberty is recognized around the world as a symbol of freedom and democracy.

CITIZENSHIP IN THE COLONIES

Although early European settlers are sometimes said to be the first Americans, in reality they were the first immigrants. Native Americans had lived in the land that is now the United States for centuries. The colonists who came over from England—and other parts of Europe—simply settled in a land that was already populated by Native Americans.

England and the colonies had charters with vague "rules" about naturalization, but the rules were rather conflicting. It was unclear whether the colonies could establish their own rules of naturalization, or whether that had to come from England.

Native Americans lived in North America long before Europeans arrived to settle.

ENGLISH SUBJECTS

When the Pilgrims settled in North America, they settled as colonists, who were still technically living under English rule—at least, according to English common law. The Pilgrims did have some freedoms they couldn't have enjoyed in England, simply because they lived thousands of miles away from the king in an era when communication was slow and unreliable. But in matters of law and citizenship, the Pilgrims were still considered subjects of the king of England.

EARLY LAWS

In the 1670s, there was a process of private naturalization. It allowed residents of the American colonies to essentially purchase English naturalization. However, it was a difficult, expensive, and somewhat arbitrary process that was influenced by xenophobia and religious prejudice.

The Plantation Act 1740 declared that any Protestant residing in the American colonies for 7 years—with no absence of greater than 2 months during that period—could be declared an English subject. But still, that was citizenship under British rule, not true American citizenship.

THE FIRST NATURALIZED AMERICANS

Probably the first true American citizenship happened in the individual colonies, when in the early eighteenth century individual naturalization laws were established. These laws were useful in the individual colonies, but not particularly useful in the rest of the world, since English rule and law still trumped the policies set forth in individual colonies. Still, it was a start. Most of the original colonies set up naturalization policies and laws—New Hampshire was the only colony that did not.

The laws generally looked a lot like naturalization laws look today. Residents were required to swear allegiance to the colony and were granted the right to vote and own land. Today's national citizenship rights and responsibilities are much more detailed, but similar basic ideas existed as the early colonies set up naturalization policies.

Even babies born in America were born as subjects of the English monarchy. They were born into the citizenship of the colony of their birth, of course, but above all they were born under English rule and law.

REVOLUTIONARY WAR CITIZENSHIP

In 1775, the Revolutionary War broke out between the American colonies and England. The colonists were tired of paying taxes to England, without enjoying all the rights of English citizens. On July 2, 1776, the Continental Congress (formed of representatives from twelve of the colonies) voted for independence. The Declaration of Independence was issued just two days later, declaring that the thirteen colonies were now thirteen independent states forming a new nation independent of Great Britain—the United States of America.

Although the Revolutionary War lasted for more than 8 years, July 4, 1776, is considered the date of birth of the United States. At that point, the colonists who had been living in America became United States citizens—a mass naturalization!

The forces of the United States triumphed over the British Army to win the Revolutionary War.

THE FIRST NATURAL-BORN U.S. CITIZENS

Once the Declaration of Independence was issued, babies born in the United States were born with U.S. citizenship. So who was first? It's impossible to say, since birth records listed dates but generally not times—and they were only as accurate as the people reporting them, since babies were born at home, not in hospitals.

However, there were several babies born in the United States on July 4, 1776. A woman named Philippa Cropley was one of the people born that day, though her exact place of birth is not known. Another baby born that day was rather appropriately named America Midyett. Ethan Allen Brown was also born in Connecticut on that day. Brown is probably the best known of the babies born that day, because he went on to serve in the Ohio Supreme Court and as governor of Ohio and as a United States senator.

The Declaration of Independence was signed by representatives from all thirteen colonies.

A NEW GOVERNMENT

Once the United States declared its independence, the Second Continental Congress began drafting the Articles of Confederation, which served as the nation's first constitution. The Articles of Confederation set forth some rules about movement and residency within the states, but the rules were not terribly clear or uniform.

When the United States Constitution became the law of the land in 1789, it attempted to establish naturalization policies. However, the policy was somewhat vague: Article I, Section Eight, of the Constitution says that Congress has the power "To establish a uniform Rule of Naturalization." It was then up to Congress to decide what those rules would be.

WHO WAS A CITIZEN?

When the Constitution was drafted, white men who owned property were the only full citizens who generally enjoyed all the rights available. Other members of the population (women, children, and minorities) did not have all the same rights given to property-owning white males.

Over the years, the Constitution has been amended numerous times. Slowly, over two centuries, naturalization laws changed. Eventually all white men (not just property owners) gained the right to vote. This was extended to black men in 1870, to women in 1920, and to people 18 or older in 1971. Other citizenship rights have also evolved, as the United States has continued to grow and change. And they will continue to change in the coming years, decades, and centuries.

The Constitution established more formal rules about citizenship in the United States.

ASIAN IMMIGRATION

Xenophobia—fear or dislike of people from foreign countries—affected naturalization from the colonies' earliest days, and it continues to affect it today. As the United States grew as a country, some immigrants were less accepted than others, because they seemed different from what U.S. citizens were familiar with at the time.

European immigrants had been coming to the United States since the colonies were under British rule. These immigrants had cultures, customs, and even languages that varied depending on their country of origin. However, they were generally white and seemed at least somewhat familiar to American citizens.

THE FIRST ASIANS ARRIVE

When large numbers of Asians began immigrating to the United States in the mid-nineteenth century, they seemed new and different. There were some Asian people in the United States from earlier, small migrations, but many Americans had never met one.

Most of the new immigrants were from China, Japan, and the Philippines. They looked different from the European immigrants that Americans at the time were used to. In addition, their language sounded strikingly different, and used a different writing system. To American citizens, they seemed very foreign.

Many of these very early immigrants in the first wave of Asian immigration settled in Hawaii, far removed from the U.S. mainland. However, the Gold Rush that began in California in 1848 brought many to the West Coast as well. In a four-year span from 1848 to 1852, the Chinese immigrant population rose from fewer than 400 to 25,000.

More Asian immigrants arrived to work in various types of labor. These immigrants were largely from Japan, Korea, and South Asia. They were often met with racism. The Asiatic Exclusion League and other organizations were formed to try to bar Asians from immigrating to America. Sadly, some Asian immigrants were even murdered.

Some of the first Asian immigrants came to Hawaii, which was not yet a U.S. state.

LAWS ON ASIAN IMMIGRATION

The United States Congress was not immune to racism. In 1875 they passed the Page Act, which barred Asian immigrants from coming to the United States for jobs in forced labor. The Page Act also made it particularly difficult for Asian women to come to the United States. In particular, it made it so essentially no Chinese women could come to the country.

Customs officials in San Francisco inspected the luggage of Chinese immigrants.

NEW LAWS

The situation got even worse in 1882 with the Chinese Exclusion Act, which prohibited nearly all immigration from China. In 1892, the Geary Act stated that all Chinese people must carry identification certificates or face being deported. There were also a number of other requirements that were oppressive to Chinese people.

Although such acts sound almost unthinkable now, history does repeat itself. The 2016 presidential election featured much discussion about a proposed "Muslim registry" where people of Muslim faith living in the United States would be required to register.

RELAXING THE RULES

Immigrants from Asia continued to arrive, but it was a slow process for Americans to warm to these immigrants. Outright anti-Asian hostility continued for decades. At the same time, new laws were passed that made it difficult for people of Asian descent to gain U.S. citizenship.

It wasn't until after World War II that immigration policies began to relax. In 1943, the Magnuson Act allowed some Chinese immigrants living in the United States to become U.S. citizens. It also created a quota that would allow 105 people from China to immigrate to the United States each year. However, these immigrants still did not have full citizenship rights. Chinese people were prevented from owning property or businesses.

THE ROAD TOWARD EQUALITY

The McCarran-Walter Act, passed in 1952, allowed for the naturalization of Asians living in the United States. However, the strict quotas on the numbers of Asian immigrants allowed each year were still in place. The Immigration and Nationality Act of 1965 finally allowed more people from Asia to immigrate to the United States by eliminating nationality-based discrimination in the immigration quotas.

Fortunately, anti-Asian sentiment has lessened in the United States, particularly in the past several decades. People of Asian descent are now as much a part of the country as anyone, and those who have obtained citizenship now enjoy the same rights as every other U.S. citizen.

INTERNMENT CAMPS

Immigration was one thing, but acceptance was another. Racism toward people of Asian descent took decades to crumble, and it was on full display during World War II. The United States was at war with Japan, and worried that Japanese Americans might be disloyal to their adopted country. In 1942, the U.S. government forced approximately 120,000 people of Japanese descent living in the United States into internment camps, where many remained until 1946.

 Japanese familes were systematically taken to detention centers and then sent to internment camps.

 Decades later, the U.S. government apologized for its treatment of Japanese Americans, and paid compensation to surviving detainees.

CHAPTER 2

INVOLUNTARY IMMIGRATION AND CITIZENSHIP

It's easy to forget that not all immigrants to the United States wanted to come. For many years America had a reputation as a "promised land" where people came from other countries to better their lives. However, it certainly wasn't like that for slaves, who were brought by force from Africa, bought by white landowners, and forced to work without pay.

Slaves were brought to North America as early as the seventeenth century. They were forced to perform many jobs without pay, including farming and developing the new land colonists were settling in. White settlers often viewed them as different and many thought they were entitled to fewer rights and poorer treatment.

By the early to mid-nineteenth century, slavery was widespread in the United States.

SLAVERY IN THE SOUTH

Slavery in North America actually began even before the Mayflower arrived from England in 1620. The year before, Dutch traders had brought 20 captured slaves from Africa to Jamestown, Virginia. The slaves were forced to work in the tobacco fields and on other large farms.

The practice of slavery continued from that time until the mid-1860s. During the eighteenth century alone, it is likely that between 6 and 7 million slaves were brought to the United States from Africa. Slavery was particularly common in the South. Slaves were used for manual labor in the cotton fields and on tobacco, rice, and indigo plantations. The South relied on slave labor to make its economy work.

SLAVERY IN THE REVOLUTIONARY WAR ERA

While the South largely depended on slave labor to maintain its economy, it was different in the North. The North's economy was able to sustain itself without slave labor, and eventually many Northerners began to question the situation in the South. They recognized that slavery wasn't so different from what their ancestors had been through before the Revolutionary War, when they were oppressed by British rule.

Slavery didn't end with the Revolutionary War, though. The Constitution recognized the existence of slavery. In fact, it specifically labeled slaves as equivalent to three-fifths of a person where taxation and congressional representation were concerned. The Naturalization Act of 1790 also recognized the existence of slavery, declaring that citizenship was available to "any alien, being a free white person who shall have resided within...the United States for the term of two years."

WORKING TOWARD ABOLITION

In the years after independence, the northern states continued to move away from slavery. By 1804, all northern states had abolished the institution. In 1808, the Act Prohibiting Importation of Slaves took effect and ordered that no new slaves could be brought into the United States. However, slaves could still be traded within the United States, so slavery continued.

In the 1830s, the abolitionist movement began to gain more support. In 1857, the Supreme Court made a landmark ruling in the Dred Scott case (Dred Scott v. Sandford). Dred Scott was a slave who tried to sue for his freedom on the basis that his owner had taken him to free states and territories. These territories had been acquired after the Revolutionary War and therefore were not necessarily subject to the rules of the U.S. Constitution. Scott lost his case when the court ruled that Scott was essentially the owner's "property," and property could not be removed from an owner. It was a hard blow for the abolitionists.

FAMOUS FACES

SOJOURNER TRUTH

In 1826, Isabella Baumfree, a slave in New York, escaped slavery with her infant daughter, Sophia, and gained her freedom. She left behind her two other children—another daughter and a son. When Baumfree learned that her son was illegally sold to a man in Alabama, she went to court and won his return.

At the time, it was almost unheard of for a black woman to win a case in a United States court. But that wasn't the only court case she won—in 1835, she also won a slander suit against a couple who tried to falsely implicate her for the murder of her former employer.

I SELL THE SHADOW TO SUPPORT THE SUBSTANCE.
SOJOURNER TRUTH.

Sojourner Truth was not only a leading abolitionist, but also an early and outspoken member of the women's rights movement.

Once her children were grown, Baumfree changed her name to Sojourner Truth, inspired by her belief that God had called upon her to go forth into the countryside and speak the word of hope. Truth became well known as an abolitionist and an activist. Her memoirs, *The Narrative of Sojourner Truth: A Northern Slave*, were published in 1850—the same year she spoke at the first National Women's Rights Convention. Throughout the Civil War and after, she worked tirelessly for reform. She died in 1883 but remains known as a leader of the abolitionist movement and an early champion of women's rights and equality.

THE CIVIL WAR

A few years after the Dred Scott decision, the Civil War broke out. It was the result of growing tensions between the northern and southern states, most notably about the institution of slavery. A new president, Abraham Lincoln, had been elected in 1860, and he supported limiting slavery. In response, eleven southern states seceded from the North to create the Confederate States of America. In their own country, they could make their own laws and continue their slave-owning practices.

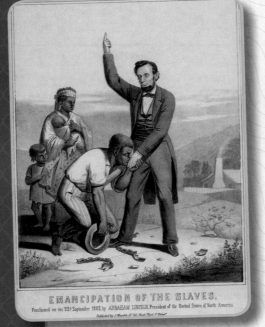

EMANCIPATION OF THE SLAVES.
Proclaimed on the 22d September 1862, by ABRAHAM LINCOLN, President of the United States of North America.

The country was plunged into a bloody civil war in which hundreds of thousands of people died. President Lincoln issued the Emancipation Proclamation in 1863, which granted slaves their freedom—but only if they were able to escape the Confederate government. This document didn't lead to a mass naturalization, like the one that occurred at the end of the Revolutionary War. Rather, if a slave could escape the Confederate government and reach free territory, then he or she was granted freedom, but not citizenship.

The Emancipation Proclamation was a major step toward freeing slaves, although it did not make them citizens.

THE THIRTEENTH AMENDMENT

The Emancipation Proclamation was a big step—but not a full step—toward citizenship. The Confederacy ultimately lost the war in 1865, and the Thirteenth Amendment to the Constitution came into effect later that year. This amendment banned slavery throughout the country, declaring that "neither slavery nor involuntary servitude, except as a punishment for crime whereof the party shall have been duly convicted, shall exist within the United States, or any place subject to their jurisdiction."

AFTER THE WAR

The Emancipation Proclamation and the Thirteenth Amendment were precursors to another major step toward citizenship: the Civil Rights Act of 1866. The act established that "all persons born in the United States" were declared citizens of the United States. This meant that children born in the United States, to parents who had been slaves, were granted citizenship. The act further defined what that citizenship meant, saying:

"Such citizens, of every race and color, and without regard to any previous condition of slavery or involuntary servitude...shall have the same right in every State and Territory in the United States... and to full and equal benefit of all laws and proceedings for the security of person and property, as is enjoyed by white citizens."

Shortly after the Emancipation Proclamation was issued, many slaves escaped north, toward the land held by the Union Army.

THE FOURTEENTH AMENDMENT

In 1868, the Fourteenth Amendment to the Constitution was ratified. It further solidified the provisions of the Civil Rights Act of 1866. The Fourteenth Amendment is composed of five sections, and the first one states that:

> "All persons born or naturalized in the United States...are citizens of the United States and of the State wherein they reside. No State shall make or enforce any law which shall abridge the privileges or immunities of citizens of the United States; nor shall any State deprive any person of life, liberty, or property, without due process of law; nor deny to any person within its jurisdiction the equal protection of the laws."

For issues of citizenship, that was the key section of the Fourteenth Amendment. Unfortunately, as iron-clad as it sounds for protecting the rights of black citizens—and all other citizens—the South found loopholes to continue racial segregation.

THE JIM CROW SOUTH

After the Civil War, the South went through a period known as Reconstruction. During this time they were supposed to revise their social and economic structure to align with a free country in which no slaves were held. By the letter of the law, they did that—slaves were all technically free in the South at that point. But the South established a "separate but equal" system of society in which black people's rights were not equal to those of whites. The state and local laws that supported this system were called Jim Crow laws. By law, slaves and their descendants were free citizens, but they still didn't enjoy the same rights as white citizens.

SEGREGATION

In the South, public schools were available to everyone, but black students couldn't go to the same schools as white students. The black schools were notoriously underfunded and staffed with teachers who didn't necessarily have training at the same level as the teachers at white schools.

 Segregation was rampant in the Jim Crow South.

In the same way, transportation was available to everyone, but black people had to sit in the back of the bus and had to give up their seats to white people if the bus was crowded. Trains had separate cars and dining facilities for black people. Restaurants were segregated into white and black. Black people couldn't even use the same drinking fountains as white people. And white employers could choose not to hire black people.

 Separate drinking fountains were a harsh reminder that black people were free, but not equal in the eyes of many Americans.

21

FREEDOM WITHOUT RIGHTS

PERSONAL STORIES

In the early to mid-twentieth century, African Americans who had been born in America or who had been naturalized were United States citizens. However, in many places they didn't have the same rights as white people. Jerry Hutchinson, who grew up in Indiana, remembers car trips to visit family in the 1950s, when they would pack an empty coffee can in the car to urinate in.

"Packing that ole coffee can was as important as any of the other items normally carried on a road trip in those days. My parents never addressed why we had to carry it. They didn't need to, because even as a child I already knew the answer to the unasked question. Ole Jim Crow didn't allow for us to use the restroom whenever we stopped for gas. That stop for fuel would be the only stop made. It just wasn't thought safe to do otherwise."

They were citizens—but not citizens who could simply stop for a bathroom break when nature called.

THE CIVIL RIGHTS ACT OF 1964

Sadly, the Jim Crow laws were not abolished until the Civil Rights Act of 1964. This law made discrimination based on race, color, religion, sex, and national origin illegal and also outlawed racial segregation at schools, workplaces, and public facilities. It was a landmark decision for the rights of black people and other groups who had faced discrimination, but even so, black citizens still didn't have full citizenship rights in all places.

For example, before 2000, marriage between mixed-race couples in the state of Alabama was banned. If a black person and a white person wanted to get married in the state, it was technically not allowed. However, the U.S. Supreme Court had declared laws like this to be unconstitutional in 1967, but several states kept them on the books. From a purely legal standpoint, black people in Alabama did not enjoy full citizenship rights at that point.

MOVING FORWARD

The path to citizenship and equal rights for black people in the United States has been very long and very slow. Thankfully, we continue to move forward, toward the goal of all people who are U.S. citizens enjoying the same rights and freedoms.

 Civil rights leader Martin Luther King Jr. looks as President Lyndon B. Johnson signs the Civil Rights Act of 1964.

CHAPTER 3

GREEN CARDS AND RESIDENCY

For people wanting to gain United States citizenship, the first step is obtaining what is known as a green card. A green card is a permit that allows a person who is a citizen of a foreign country to live and work permanently in the United States. The card's formal name is the United States Permanent Resident Card.

"Green card" is just an informal name for the card. They actually are green in color, though they haven't always been. They were green from 1946 until 1964, and then again from 2010 to the present. But "green card" rolls off the tongue much better than their real name, so almost everyone calls them that—including the U.S. Citizenship and Immigration Services website!

Green cards haven't always been green—but the name has still stuck!

TYPES OF GREEN CARDS

There are two types of green cards. The most common is a permanent green card, which is valid for ten years before needing renewal. The other type, a conditional green card, is less common. They are only valid for two years. Conditional green cards are usually issued to new spouses of United States citizens and K-1 visa holders (fiancé[e]s of United States citizens). This helps avoid situations in which an immigrant marries a U.S. citizen for the sole purpose of gaining United States citizenship.

If an immigrant holds a conditional green card, he or she must apply to have the conditions removed 90 days prior to when the card is set to expire. If the request is granted, the immigrant will then be granted a permanent green card.

BENEFITS OF HAVING A GREEN CARD

So why would an immigrant want a green card? First, it allows them to apply for many more jobs. Most employers require employees to complete an I-9 form for employment eligibility, and the green card is used to prove employment eligibility. With a green card, an immigrant is eligible to work in almost any job in the United States, except for a few jobs where top-level security clearance is required.

Second, a green card allows an immigrant to apply for a driver's license and Social Security card—both important pieces of documentation for anyone living in the United States. In addition to being a useful photo ID, a driver's license is obviously required if the individual wants to drive while living in the United States.

MORE BENEFITS

A green card also gives an immigrant many legal rights he or she would not otherwise have. Immigrants holding green cards are eligible for tax benefits, research grants, insurance and Social Security benefits, education sponsorship at the state level, and retirement benefits. Additionally, immigrants holding green cards can legally own homes and other property, cars, and firearms in the United States.

A green card also allows an immigrant to travel outside the United States for up to one year without requiring a reentry permit when returning to the U.S. Since getting a reentry permit isn't guaranteed, having a green card provides a way around that obstacle if an immigrant wants to travel outside of the United States.

Another important benefit is that a green card allows an immigrant to sponsor family members. This helps them obtain their own green cards and come to live and work in the United States. However, the most important benefit to many immigrants is that a green card allows them to eventually seek United States citizenship.

GETTING A GREEN CARD THROUGH FAMILY CONNECTIONS

One of the ways that immigrants get green cards is through family connections. If an immigrant is an immediate relative of a United States citizen, they may obtain a green card through that connection. Husbands, wives, parents, or unmarried children under the age of 21 are all considered immediate relatives.

 The rules around green cards are designed to help keep families together whenever possible.

Exceptions are sometimes made for unmarried children over the age of 21, married children of any age, or siblings age 21 or older. In addition, if an immigrant has a family member who is not a United States citizen but who holds a valid green card, the immigrant may be able to obtain a green card through that connection as well.

There are also some special categories for family members that may allow immigrants to obtain a green card. These include battered children or spouses, children born to foreign diplomats in the United States, widows or widowers of U.S. citizens, and fiancé(e)s of U.S. citizens and their minor children (through K Nonimmigrant status). There are also categories for people who have obtained a V visa. This visa allows the spouse and/or children of a U.S. resident to live and work in the United States while they are waiting to earn immigrant status.

EMPLOYMENT-BASED GREEN CARDS

An immigrant may be granted a green card on the basis of employment. Immigrants who receive permanent job offers in the United States are eligible for green cards. The technology field is particularly well known for attracting talented employees from other countries, bringing an influx of immigrants into areas where tech businesses are clustered.

Even if an immigrant doesn't have a permanent job offer, he or she may still be able to get a green card by petitioning U.S. Citizenship and Immigration Services on the basis of extraordinary ability or national interest. Foreign entrepreneurs or investors may also be granted a green card, if they are investing in or starting an enterprise that is expected to create new jobs in the United States.

There are also certain specific job categories under which an immigrant can be issued a green card. Afghan or Iraqi translators, or Iraqis who assisted the U.S. government, fall into these categories. So do broadcasters, Panama Canal employees, religious workers, and some doctors. Some employees of international organizations are also eligible.

Immigrants with skills that are needed in the United States may be able to get a green card on the basis of employment.

ASYLUM AND REFUGEE STATUS

One of the more controversial ways to obtain a green card is through asylum or refugee status. People seeking political asylum or refuge from a dangerous or war-torn country can apply for a green card after they have been in the United States for one year. Refugees must apply for a green card when their first year in the United States ends, while it is optional (but encouraged) for those seeking asylum.

 Refugees and asylees are often a controversial issue in the United States.

Among United States citizens, the views toward refugees are mixed. Some feel the United States should be a place of refuge for those fleeing war and persecution. In recent years, these refugees have included many from Syria and the Middle East. Other Americans fear that opening the door to refugees can also allow terrorists to more easily slip in unnoticed. It's a topic that got much attention during and after the 2016 presidential election.

THE GREEN CARD LOTTERY

The green card lottery is more formally known as the Diversity Immigrant Visa Program, and it is administered by the U.S. Department of State. Each year, the department randomly selects up to 50,000 immigrants from countries with low rates of immigration to the United States and grants them visas.

THE LIFE ACT

LIFE stands for the Legal Immigration and Family Equity Act amendments of 2000. This act is one that can allow undocumented immigrants to potentially gain a green card. Under the act, a green card can be issued regardless of the manner in which the immigrant entered the country. It doesn't matter whether they were working in the United States without authorization, or whether they had maintained lawful status since entering the United States.

To be eligible under the LIFE Act, the immigrant must be the beneficiary of a qualified immigrant petition or application for labor certification filed before May 1, 2001. They must also have been physically present in the United States on December 21, 2000, if their petition was filed between January 15, 1998, and April 30, 2001. In addition, they must have a visa immediately available, and must be admissible to the United States.

SPECIAL IMMIGRANT JUVENILE STATUS

The Special Immigrant Juvenile program is designed for foreign-born children in the United States who have been abused, neglected, or abandoned. Under this program, these children can get a green card to live and work permanently in the United States, but they may never petition for a green card for their parents, and they cannot petition for a green card for their siblings until they have become naturalized United States citizens.

OTHER GREEN CARD PROGRAMS

There are some other programs under which an immigrant can obtain a green card. Civilian North Atlantic Treaty Organization (NATO) employees and their spouses and unmarried children are eligible for green cards, as are Native Americans born in Canada, and Cuban natives and citizens. Haitian refugees may also obtain green cards if they meet certain eligibility requirements. Many Amerasian children were fathered by American soldiers during the Korean and Vietnam wars, and U.S. Citizenship and Immigration Services has a program under which those children can obtain a green card.

Foreign citizens who have assisted United States law enforcement as a witness or informant are also eligible for a green card. So are certain parolees and refugees from countries where they were persecuted, including countries making up the former Soviet Union and some Asian nations. Victims of human trafficking are eligible for green cards as well. Finally, there is a program in place for people who have resided in the United States since before 1972, even if they entered illegally.

Many Cubans have been issued green cards that allow them to immigrate to the United States.

NO GUARANTEES

As you can see, there are many categories and programs under which a person can gain a green card and become a permanent resident of the United States. However, that does not mean that every person who falls into one or more of those categories will be granted a green card. Each category has criteria an immigrant must meet to be considered for a green card, and the immigrant must provide all of the necessary evidence and documentation to prove he or she meets the eligibility requirements. It is not a simple process—but some say that for people seeking a permanent life in the United States, it is worth the effort.

PERSONAL STORIES

ACTORS WHO IMMIGRATED

A number of well-known actors and actresses have come to the United States under green cards. Audrey Hepburn, the star of the 1961 movie *Breakfast at Tiffany's* and other movies, came to the United States from the United Kingdom, but she was originally born in Belgium. She was also a British citizen and went to school in England as a child. However, her family moved to the Netherlands during World War II. Hepburn immigrated to the United States in 1951.

Audrey Hepburn became famous as a Hollywood star, though she was actually European.

RESPONSIBILITIES OF GREEN CARD HOLDERS

Being granted a green card comes with certain responsibilities. Green card holders must obey all federal, state, and local laws. Like any United States citizen, they must file income tax and pay the appropriate state and federal taxes. They must also vow to support the United States' democratic government and not try to change the government structure through illegal means. And finally, if they are male and between the ages of 18 and 25, they must register with Selective Service, which means in a military draft situation, they could be called upon to serve in the United States military.

Mila Kunis is proof that religious persecution is still a very real problem for people in some countries.

Actress Mila Kunis was born in Ukraine. As a child, she and her family immigrated to avoid persecution. Kunis and her Jewish family faced persecution in Ukraine due to their beliefs, so the family came to the United States in 1991, when Mila was 7 years old.

Comedian and actor Will Arnett immigrated to the United States from Canada to pursue a career in 1990 and has lived in the United States ever since. Around the same time, Spanish actor Antonio Banderas emigrated from Spain to pursue a film career in Hollywood after gaining fame in his native country.

CHAPTER 4

ELIGIBILITY FOR CITIZENSHIP

Some green card holders are content to remain permanent legal residents of the United States. But many others want to take it a step further, and be naturalized as a United States citizen. Becoming a citizen means taking a full part in the life of their adopted country. It gives a person certain rights and responsibilities, so it isn't a decision to be taken lightly. And it isn't exactly an easy process. There are many eligibility requirements a person must meet before an application for citizenship will even be considered.

AGE

Applicants for citizenship must be at least 18 years old. There are several different citizenship rules for people under the age of 18, depending on whether their parents are U.S. citizens. If the parents are part of the United States military, the rules may be different. But for the average person, 18 is the age at which one can seek United States citizenship.

RESIDENCY

For an adult to obtain United States citizenship, the first step is establishing residency. In general, adults over the age of 18 must have held a green card and resided continuously in the United States for five years before they can apply for naturalization. There is a slight loophole for adults who are married to U.S. citizens—they only have to have resided in the United States with a green card for three years before they can apply for naturalization. There is also an expedited path to citizenship for military families.

WAYNE GRETZKY

Hockey star Wayne Gretzky has been nicknamed "the Great One" because he is believed to be one of the best hockey players in history. In a long career, spent mainly with the Edmonton Oilers and the Los Angeles Kings, he set many National Hockey League records, and still holds 60 of them. One of his greatest achievements was becoming the only player to score more than 200 points in a single season.

But the NHL's greatest star wasn't originally from the United States. He was born in Canada and remains a Canadian citizen to this day. However, he holds dual citizenship. He gained his U.S. citizenship after he married American actress Janet Jones and went to live in Los Angeles in 1988, to take up a position with the Los Angeles Kings.

There are no official statistics on dual citizenship, but Wayne Gretzky is one of many people who are citizens of the United States and another country.

CONTINUOUS RESIDENCY

For most adults seeking naturalization, they must have resided in the United States with a green card for at least five years immediately preceding their application. In other words, an adult cannot live for five years in the United States, then go live in a foreign country for a year and then return to the United States and apply for citizenship. The time of residence must be immediately before the application is filed.

The applicant must also be physically present in the United States for at least 30 of the 60 months that make up the five-year residency period. For people who travel extensively, this requirement can pose a bit of a challenge. Their legal residence may be in a particular U.S. state for five years, but if they've been out of the country for more than 30 months during that period, they will not be eligible for naturalization.

Immigration law is incredibly complex, and the laws change frequently.

A ROADBLOCK ON THE PATH TO CITIZENSHIP

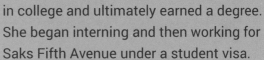

Rebeca De Vives from Chile got an unexpected surprise when she tried to become a United States citizen: a deportation order!

Rebeca had been living in the United States since she was 22 years old. She followed her husband, a doctor, when he came to do his training in pediatrics at Children's Hospital in Boston. Rebeca's English was poor, so she found a job as a babysitter—a job that didn't require her to be fluent in English. As her English skills improved, she enrolled in college and ultimately earned a degree. She began interning and then working for Saks Fifth Avenue under a student visa.

After five years at Saks, Rebeca and her husband decided to apply for citizenship. Her husband's was granted with no problem, but Rebeca's was not—instead, she faced deportation in 15 days. Apparently, all her work at Saks had been under a temporary work permit, which she hadn't renewed each time she left and returned to the country—a requirement she was unaware of.

Rebeca's story has a happy ending: her attorney father in Madrid, Spain, was able to process a permanent visa for her, so she was able to return to the United States and continue her life there. But it was quite a wake-up call to Rebeca when she faced nearly immediate deportation because of a simple mistake!

STATE RESIDENCY

An applicant must have lived within the state or U.S. Citizenship and Immigration Services jurisdiction for at least three months before filing an application. If a person wants to file for citizenship in New York City, for example, then he or she must live in New York City for at least three months before filing the application.

The exception to this is university students. Many students go to a college or university in a different state from where their parents live. In these cases, students can file for citizenship either where they go to school or where their parents live—if they are not yet financially independent from their parents. If they are financially independent from their parents, then they must file in the state or jurisdiction where they go to school.

DURING THE APPLICATION PROCESS

Once a person has filed an application for naturalization (which is done on Form N-400), they must reside continuously in the United States up until they are officially granted United States citizenship. They cannot file an application and then leave to live in another country while they wait for their citizenship to be approved.

KNOWLEDGE AND CHARACTER

To be considered for citizenship, a person must demonstrate both general knowledge and strong character. This might seem rather vague, but it's actually fairly well defined by U.S. Citizenship and Immigration Services. When it comes to the knowledge criterion, applicants for citizenship must be able to speak, read, and write in English. They must also possess some basic knowledge of United States history and government.

For immigrant children who have grown up going to U.S. schools, these eligibility requirements usually aren't a problem—English is the main language taught in all United States schools, and students take history and government classes throughout their school career.

The Armenian community in Los Angeles comes together to mark important dates and events for their culture.

HARDER FOR SOME

These particular eligibility requirements may be slightly more challenging for adult immigrants who didn't grow up going to U.S. schools. There are places in the United States where immigrants can live and speak their native language without ever having to learn English. For example, there are parts of the Los Angeles area that are commonly referred to as "Little Armenia" because many Armenian immigrants have settled there. Members of the older generation don't necessarily speak any English. For immigrants like these, the knowledge requirements for citizenship may pose a real challenge.

GOOD MORAL CHARACTER

Applicants for naturalization must demonstrate that they have a strong moral character, and that they support the principles of the U.S. Constitution. This might also seem vague: how does a person prove that they are of good moral character? Isn't that a rather debatable issue?

Earning U.S. citizenship is a long process, but for many immigrants, it is definitely worth it.

Say that an immigrant stole some food when he arrived in the country because he couldn't afford to feed his family, but then once he got a job, his record was clean. Would that be an example of poor moral character because he stole? Or would it be good moral character because he was providing for his family? A good lawyer could argue either way, and the person's punishment would no doubt depend somewhat on how well the lawyer argued either side.

Thankfully, the U.S. Citizenship and Immigration Services have clearly defined their standards for this criterion. Their regulations spell out various types of criminal conduct that would make a person ineligible for citizenship.

LANGUAGE BARRIERS

Language was a stumbling block for Celia and Alfredo Ramirez, a couple who immigrated to the United States from Mexico in 1998. Celia had a green card, while Alfredo had a tourist visa. As soon as they were eligible to apply for citizenship, they both did. Unfortunately, they were both denied because they didn't meet the English language proficiency criteria.

It was a disappointing blow to the Ramirezes, but they reapplied for citizenship in 2016—this time with help. The East Bay Naturalization Collaborative in the San Francisco Bay Area, an organization that provides help for people seeking citizenship, came to their aid.

By this point, Celia and Alfredo were old enough to take advantage of a language exemption. There are 50/20 and 55/15 language exemptions, which mean that immigrants are exempt from the language requirement if they are over the age of 50 and have lived as a permanent resident in the United States for 20 years, or they are over the age of 55 and have lived in the country as a permanent resident for 15 years. The East Bay Naturalization Collaborative helped the Ramirezes secure the exemption and then worked with them to prepare for the rest of the application process. It took 18 years, but the Ramirezes were finally able to enjoy the same rights as all other American citizens.

ALBERT EINSTEIN

Nobel Prize–winning physicist Albert Einstein was one of the most famous naturalized United States citizens. He was born in the German Empire in 1879, but gave up his German citizenship in 1896 to avoid mandatory military service. He became a Swiss citizen in 1901, and he retained that citizenship for the rest of his life. However, he also gained United States citizenship in 1940, seven years after he and his second wife, Elsa, emigrated to the United States. By this point he had already won the coveted Nobel Prize, and presumably the United States was happy to offer citizenship to such an acclaimed person!

PERSONAL STORIES

Einstein moved to the United States in 1933 when Hitler came to power in Germany.

CRIMINAL ACTS

In general, if a person stays on the right side of the law, the character eligibility requirements are relatively easy to meet. However, committing certain criminal acts makes someone permanently unable to be granted U.S. citizenship. These acts include murder, aggravated felonies, persecution, genocide, torture, and severe violations of religious freedom.

Other criminal acts are only bars to gaining citizenship if they take place during the statutory period before citizenship is approved. This usually means the five years preceding the application, although if a person is the spouse of a U.S. citizen or is a member of the U.S. military, the statutory period may vary. These acts include personal and property crimes, drug offenses, human trafficking, giving false testimony, gambling offenses, repeated drunkenness, failure to pay child support as ordered, and being imprisoned for 180 days or more.

EXCEPTIONS

There are a few exceptions where moral character is concerned. First, a simple arrest cannot usually be held against an immigrant's moral character—there must be a conviction for the offense to count against the person's moral character. In this case, conviction is defined as a formal judgment of guilt entered by a court.

Second, juvenile convictions don't usually count against a person's moral character for immigration purposes. The exception to this exception is if a juvenile was charged as an adult for a crime and was ultimately convicted of that crime. Also, foreign convictions will only count as convictions for U.S. immigration purposes if the foreign conviction was for something that is also against the law in the United States. Expunged records, vacated judgments, and pardoned offenses also do not generally count against an immigrant's good moral character.

CHAPTER 5

THE NATURALIZATION TEST AND PROCESS

Once a person has met all of the requirements to become a United States citizen, it is time for the next step. They can fill out the necessary application and then proceed through the testing and interview process. The first step is filling out Form N-400.

APPLICATION FOR NATURALIZATION

Form N-400 is the Application for Naturalization, provided by the U.S. Citizenship and Immigration Services. This 20-page form requires a lot of information and documentation to be submitted. It is broken down into sections. The first sections cover eligibility requirements and personal information, such as address, age, and residency.

U.S. Citizenship and Immigration Services provides the forms that immigrants must fill out to apply for citizenship.

Later sections ask questions about the applicant's parents, and about his or her life before the application. Applicants must provide information about their education and the jobs they have had. They also have to list any times during their statutory period where they were outside of the United States. A section on family covers any marriages, divorces, and children.

For a fluent speaker of English, the form is relatively simple to fill out, although long and tedious. However, for an immigrant who has not yet mastered English, the form may be challenging, which is why it's not unusual for someone to assist the applicant with filling out the application.

 ## A BOY WITHOUT A COUNTRY

PERSONAL STORIES

UCLA law professor Hiroshi Motomura became a naturalized American citizen at the age of 15. While many immigrants renounce citizenship from their home country to become American citizens, Motomura was a unique case: he was a boy without a country. According to his naturalization certificate, he was considered "stateless."

Motomura came to the United States from Japan when he was three years old. His father was an American citizen but hadn't lived in the United States for long enough before Motomura's birth to give him U.S. citizenship. And Motomura couldn't be considered a Japanese citizen because only his mother was Japanese, and up until the 1980s citizenship in Japan passed through the father, not the mother.

It wasn't guaranteed that the stateless Motomura would be granted U.S. citizenship, even though he had lived in the country since childhood. Rather, Motomura says, "Somewhere along the line I became American. It wasn't some single moment or anything like that. But now I think I really am. And I guess I'm really not going back."

NEXT STEPS

Once the application form is complete, the applicant must submit it along with two passport-style photographs, all supporting documentation, and the required biometric services fees. Then U.S. Citizenship and Immigration Services will schedule a biometrics appointment for the individual.

WHAT ARE BIOMETRICS?

"Biometrics" is a term for the physical data that can be used to identify a person. This could be fingerprints, a photo, or other records such as a retinal scan. In today's high-tech world, data like these can be crucial to proving your identity. The U.S. Citizenship and Immigration Services collect fingerprints, a photograph, and a digital signature from each applicant for citizenship. They use this data to create an individual profile on their system, and also to check that criminals are not making a fraudulent application.

Even people just visiting the United States from other countries often have to provide biometric data.

THE BIOMETRICS APPOINTMENT

An applicant's biometrics appointment usually occurs three to four months after Form N-400 is filed, and a few weeks before the naturalization interview. The biometrics appointment takes place at one of the many Application Support Centers located around the United States. For rural areas and for military personnel, applicants can sometimes get an appointment at a mobile biometrics van, rather than traveling to the nearest large city.

Gathering the data doesn't take long—generally around 20 minutes or so. However, waiting times can be long. Once the appointment is finished, U.S. Citizenship and Immigration Services will stamp the applicant's appointment notice to serve as a record for the applicant that he or she did indeed attend.

The applicant's fingerprints are sent to the Federal Bureau of Investigation (FBI) to be checked against criminal databases and records of people who have tried to cross the border illegally in the past. This generally takes about three to four weeks. After the FBI has cleared the prints, U.S. Citizenship and Immigration Services will contact the applicant to schedule the naturalization interview.

BIOMETRICS EXCEPTIONS

There are some exceptions to the rules about biometrics appointments. If an applicant has previously been fingerprinted at a United States consulate or military installation, they will not need to be fingerprinted again. People applying for political asylum aren't required to pay the biometrics fees, and neither are people applying under the Family Unity Program. Also, parents and other adults in the household of a family seeking to adopt a child from another country must all be fingerprinted and pay individual biometrics fees.

SCHEDULING AN INTERVIEW

The next step after the biometrics appointment is the naturalization interview, which will be scheduled once U.S. Citizenship and Immigration Services receives notification from the FBI that an applicant has cleared the fingerprint background check. The fingerprints taken at the biometrics appointment are only considered valid for 15 months, so if the naturalization interview takes place more than 15 months after the biometrics appointment, the applicant may be asked to resubmit his or her fingerprints.

THE NATURALIZATION INTERVIEW

The naturalization interview will be conducted at a specified U.S. Citizenship and Immigration Services office. At the interview, the applicant will be expected to answer questions about the Form N-400 that he or she submitted. This is also the time when most applicants will take the English and civics tests, although some will be exempt from testing. If an applicant wishes to be considered exempt from testing and has not already submitted Form N-648, Medical Certification for Disability Exceptions, then he or she must submit the form at the naturalization interview.

WAITING FOR RESULTS

Some applicants will be informed of their interview results immediately after the interview. However, in some cases the U.S. Citizenship and Immigration Services officer cannot make a decision the same day—perhaps due to missing evidence or documentation, or perhaps because the applicant failed the English or civics test. If that happens, the officer will continue the case, and the applicant may be asked to provide more documentation, along with Form N-14 (Request for Additional Information, Documents, or Forms).

If an applicant fails the English or civics test (or both!), U.S. Citizenship and Immigration Services will schedule another interview in two to three months. The applicant can then retake the test he or she failed. However, each applicant is only granted one retake per test. If the applicant fails the test a second time, his or her application for citizenship will be denied.

PASS/FAIL

Most immigrants who come to the United States to work in the tech field come under an H-1B visa. With this type of visa, a United States employer has offered a job to a potential immigrant and intends for that person to have continued employment with the company.

Other immigrants enter the country under an EB-1 visa. "EB" stands for "extraordinary ability," and the immigrant has to be able to prove that he or she has extraordinary ability in some certain field. Often this is reserved for people in the arts, but it can also be applied to technology fields.

 Naturalization ceremonies are incredibly momentous events for those who are granted citizenship.

THE NATURALIZATION TEST

Part of the naturalization interview includes taking the naturalization test. The naturalization test has two parts: one is on the English language, and the other part is on civics, which covers basic information about U.S. history and government, as well as the rights and duties of citizens.

The English portion of the test covers reading, writing, and speaking. An applicant's speaking ability is assessed during the naturalization interview. During the test, the applicant must correctly read one out of three sentences. They must also write out one out of three sentences correctly. For applicants who have gone through U.S. schools, passing the test is generally relatively simple. But for older immigrants who may not have gone to English-speaking schools, it may be more challenging.

The civics test is composed of 100 possible questions. Applicants are asked up to ten questions of those 100, and they must answer six correctly to pass the test. The questions and answers must be given in English during the naturalization interview.

HOW TO PREPARE

Study materials are offered for both tests. They are available on the U.S. Citizenship and Immigration Services website. The practice materials for the English test include vocabulary flashcards, vocabulary lists, videos, and interactive self-tests. The practice materials for the civics test include question-and-answer documents in English, Spanish, and Chinese, audio Q&A programs, civics flashcards, videos, study booklets, and interactive tests.

Studying is important for immigrants who want to pass the naturalization test.

President Donald Trump greets his Secretary of Defense, James Mattis. Knowing the roles of Cabinet officials can help immigrants pass the naturalization test.

TOO SMART FOR THE TEST?

For someone who attended U.S. schools and speaks fluent English, the English and civics tests are usually not particularly difficult. But an English-speaking Canadian found that one unanticipated challenge of studying for the civics test is when the test materials are incorrect! Dafna Linzer, a reporter for ProPublica, found a number of inaccuracies in the study materials issued by U.S. Citizenship and Immigration Services.

Many of the errors were subtle issues on questions that most test-takers could easily answer despite the inaccuracy, but some were more profound. For example, one question asked the applicant to name two members of the president's Cabinet, and an expected correct answer was "vice president." Technically, the vice president is not a member of the Cabinet because he is an elected official, not an appointed head of an executive department. In other words, an applicant studying for the test should use the study materials with a bit of caution and a careful eye!

TAKING THE OATH

If an applicant passes all stages of the naturalization process, he or she is then eligible to take the Oath of Allegiance. Sometimes, applicants can take the Oath of Allegiance on the same day as their naturalization interview. However, if that is not an option, U.S. Citizenship and Immigration Services will send the applicant a notification of the scheduled oath ceremony in which the applicant is eligible to participate. This ceremony is not optional. Immigrants must take the Oath of Allegiance to be officially declared a United States citizen and granted all the rights that go along with citizenship.

AT THE CEREMONY

Either a judge or a U.S. Citizenship and Immigration Services official will preside over the naturalization ceremony, depending on the ceremony and location. Applicants must complete Form N-445, Notice of Naturalization Oath Ceremony, and bring it to the oath ceremony, where an immigration officer will review it.

An applicant must also bring his or her green card to turn in at the ceremony. After the ceremony, they will no longer need it!

Green cards are a thing of the past once an immigrant has gone through the naturalization ceremony!

RESPONSIBILITIES AND RIGHTS OF U.S. CITIZENS

Once a person has earned U.S. citizenship, he or she takes on the same responsibilities as any other U.S. citizen. According to U.S. Citizenship and Immigration Services, the key responsibilities include the following:

- *Supporting and defending the U.S. Constitution*
- *Staying informed of issues that affect their community and participating in that community*
- *Participating in the democratic process*
- *Respecting and obeying all laws at the local, state, and federal levels*
- *Paying taxes to federal, state, and local authorities*
- *Respecting other people's rights, beliefs, and opinions*
- *Performing jury service when summoned*
- *Defending the United States if the need arises*

In addition, a U.S. citizen earns the rights enjoyed by other U.S. citizens, including the following:

- *Freedom of expression*
- *Freedom to worship*
- *Right to a fair, prompt trial by a jury of one's peers*
- *Right to vote in elections*
- *Right to apply for federal employment that requires U.S. citizenship*
- *Right to run for elected office*
- *Freedom of life, liberty, and the pursuit of happiness*

CHAPTER 6

LOSS OF UNITED STATES CITIZENSHIP

Gaining U.S. citizenship is a long and difficult process, but in a few rare cases it is not permanent. It is possible for citizens—either natural-born or naturalized—to lose their citizenship, or to voluntarily give it up. It is also possible for an immigrant who is living in the United States under a green card to lose the citizenship status covered under the green card.

LOSING A GREEN CARD

It's relatively difficult for an immigrant to lose U.S. citizenship once he or she has become naturalized, but it's fairly easy to lose green-card status. Immigrants living in the U.S. can have their green card revoked for several infractions. In fact, any violation of U.S. law can be cause for revocation of a green card—even misdemeanor offenses, such as domestic violence or drug possession.

People living in the United States under a green card are encouraged to contact an immigration lawyer immediately upon arrest if they wish to avoid deportation. Some of the possible violations aren't even criminal issues. For example, immigrants are required to notify U.S. Citizenship and Immigration Services within ten days of moving to a new address. A failure to do so can result in deportation.

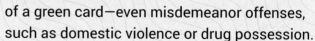

 People who are in danger of losing their green card status are advised to contact an immigration lawyer immediately.

LIVING OUTSIDE THE UNITED STATES

Many immigrants go back and forth between their birth country (or another country) and the United States. This is allowed, but immigrants living in the United States under a green card must be sure that their official place of residence remains the United States. If the government suspects that an immigrant has abandoned his or her U.S. residence, that person's green card can be revoked.

There is no set limit on the length of time an immigrant can be out of the United States before the government decides he or she has abandoned the U.S. However, a year is a good estimate—if an immigrant leaves the United States for a year or more, the government is likely to look upon it as a possible abandonment of residence. Naturally, an immigrant will have a chance to argue their case for why they left the United States for so long. Even so, there is no guarantee that the U.S. government will accept their explanation and allow them to keep their green card.

 Green card holders can travel outside the United States, but they must make sure to keep the U.S. as their official place of residence.

55

LOSING CITIZENSHIP

If a person has become a naturalized United States citizen, he or she can live outside of the United States for any length of time and still not have their citizenship revoked. That person has earned all the rights and privileges of any natural-born American citizen, and so limits on things like the amount of time spent outside the United States no longer apply. However, there are a few ways in which a citizen can lose his or her citizenship.

DENATURALIZATION

If United States immigration authorities revoke a naturalized citizen's citizenship, it is called "denaturalization." This happens when it is determined that the person gained his or her citizenship illegally, through fraud or misrepresentation. This is not a common occurrence, but it can occasionally happen. It is in an immigrant's best interest to be completely honest throughout the application process to avoid this possibility.

OTHER WAYS TO LOSE CITIZENSHIP

A naturalized citizen (or even a natural-born citizen) can also lose citizenship by voluntarily undertaking one of a list of activities. The word "voluntarily" is key here—if the person is found to have undertaken any of these activities against his or her will, then citizenship will not be revoked.

If a citizen is over 18 years of age and voluntarily becomes a naturalized citizen of another country, that person's United States citizenship may be revoked. For that to happen, they must intend to give up their U.S. nationality when being naturalized as a citizen of another country. However, in practice, many U.S. citizens are naturalized in other countries while still keeping their U.S. citizenship as well.

SERVING A FOREIGN COUNTRY

If a person joins the military in a foreign state, he or she may lose United States citizenship if the foreign military is engaged in hostilities against the United States. People serving as a commissioned or noncommissioned officer in the foreign military may also lose their U.S. citizenship.

A person over the age of 18 who accepts and performs the duties of any office or post in a foreign government can also have his or her citizenship revoked. This may happen if they take a high-level post in the foreign government. Even if they take a lower-ranking post, they may still lose their citizenship if it was their intent to give it up.

 It is sometimes legal for U.S. citizens to serve in a foreign military, but not if that country is fighting against the United States.

RENOUNCING CITIZENSHIP

People who file a formal oath of renunciation of their United States citizenship obviously lose their citizenship. There are a few reasons why U.S. citizens might do this. For some wealthy people, it's a way to get out of paying U.S. taxes. In other cases, people want to live in another country and enjoy its citizenship, but that country may not allow for dual citizenship.

DUAL CITIZENSHIP

Dual citizenship is exactly what it sounds like: a person holding dual citizenship has citizenship in two countries and enjoys all the rights and privileges that go along with being a citizen in both countries. Some people are born into dual citizenship—for example, if United States citizens travel to a foreign country that recognizes dual citizenship and they give birth to a baby while in that foreign country, the baby may have both U.S. citizenship and citizenship in the country where he or she was born.

In some cases, people are born United States citizens but later acquire nationality in another country without renouncing their U.S. citizenship. The United States government doesn't forbid this, but they do not encourage it because it can create situations in which dual nationals are faced with the obligations of one country conflicting with the laws in the other.

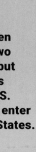

A dual citizen may have two passports, but must always use their U.S. passport to enter the United States.

TREASON

Treason and other acts against the United States government are grounds for loss of citizenship. Examples of such treasonous acts include attempting to overthrow the government, bearing arms against the United States, inciting war on the United States, participating in a subversive group (such as ISIS or al-Qaeda), or violating certain sections of the United States Code.

 ## HENRY JAMES

Henry James, the famous novelist who wrote *The Portrait of a Lady* and the novellas *Daisy Miller* and *The Turn of the Screw*, renounced his United States citizenship and began the process of becoming a British citizen in 1915. James had lived abroad since the late 1860s but had retained his United States citizenship until 1915. Although he did not confirm it at the time, many people suspected that his renunciation of citizenship was in protest of the actions (or lack thereof) of the American government. World War I was raging in Europe, and James felt strongly that the United States should take a stand against human rights violations taking place.

Henry James willingly gave up his U.S. citizenship.

PERSONAL STORIES

EFFECTS OF LOSING CITIZENSHIP

If a person loses United States citizenship—either voluntarily or involuntarily—it may be impossible to regain it. And even if the person has no intention of ever attempting to regain U.S. citizenship at a later date, the loss of it is not something to be taken lightly, as it has far-reaching consequences.

If a person's U.S. citizenship is revoked, the revocation is effective as of the date citizenship was obtained. Even if a person has been a naturalized citizen for 20 or 30 years, if that person loses citizenship, the loss is effective as of the date of naturalization, two or three decades earlier.

EFFECTS ON FAMILY MEMBERS

If a person's citizenship is revoked, their spouse or children may have their citizenship revoked as well. It depends on several factors, including whether the spouse or child resides in the United States when the citizenship is revoked and what the basis of the revocation was.

Also, if the person's spouse or children had not yet obtained citizenship at the time when the person in question's citizenship was revoked, the spouse and children can no longer gain citizenship by virtue of being the spouse or child of a naturalized United States citizen.

When a person's citizenship is revoked, his or her family members may face difficulties in gaining citizenship. »

Children of naturalized parents may lose their U.S. citizenship if they are currently living outside of the United States and it is found that their parent's citizenship was revoked on the basis of being involved in a terrorist organization or totalitarian party. This can also happen if the parent's citizenship was revoked because of a dishonorable discharge from the United States military.

REGAINING LOST CITIZENSHIP

Regaining lost citizenship is difficult, but it can occasionally be done by appealing to the State Department. However, it is unlikely that a person's citizenship would be regained if the person served in a foreign government, committed treason or otherwise acted in an anti-United States manner, or formally renounced his or her citizenship. Reinstatement is far more likely if citizenship was lost due to a mistake, such as when a person intends to hold dual citizenship and a misunderstanding leads to his or her U.S. citizenship being revoked.

For many people, acquiring U.S. citizenship is a goal that they have worked long and hard to achieve. Becoming a citizen allows them to take a full part in life in the United States. They will do as much as they can to avoid losing such a status.

GLOSSARY

abolitionist movement A movement to end slavery and ensure equal rights for blacks in the United States.

Amerasian A person with one Asian and one American parent; especially one who was born in Asia to an Asian mother and a father in the U.S. military.

dishonorable discharge A discharge given when a member of the military has been convicted by court-martial of a serious offense.

dual nationals People who are nationals of two countries simultaneously. Dual nationalism is similar to dual citizenship, but dual nationals will not necessarily hold official citizenship in both countries.

expunged records Records that are completely erased.

forced labor Work that people are forced to do under the threat of punishment.

indigo A tropical plant that is the source of a dark blue dye.

Jim Crow laws Local and state laws that enforced racial segregation after the Civil War and the Reconstruction Era.

NATO (stands for North Atlantic Treaty Organization) An association of North American and European countries formed in 1949 as a means of defense against the Soviet Union.

naturalization Admittance of someone from a foreign country to the citizenship of another country.

pardoned offenses Offenses that have been legally forgiven.

political asylum Protection for a person who has left his or her native country as a political refugee.

totalitarian A dictatorial, centralized type of government.

vacated judgment A canceled or annulled judgment.

xenophobia Fear or hatred of people from other countries.